Awakenings

Awakenings
Sacred Meditations 2006 – 2017

Dominique Vincenz

e. enlightenment books

ISBN-13: 978-0692917183 (enlightenment books)
ISBN-10: 0692917187

Cover art: Shirley Wiebe (shirleywiebe.com)
Book design: Radicle Designs
Author photo: Joe Borrelli (joeborrelli.com)
Fonts: Gill Sans, Garamond

Printed in the United States of America

First printing

*For Michael and Alexandra, my greatest teachers
and with deep gratitude to Swan, my teacher and mentor;
and—of course, all the Sacred Rebels*

I. What Gives You Life

II. Through the Wilderness

III. Midlife

IV. In the Space of Solitude

V. Open to the Not-Knowing

VI. The Elephant in the Room

VII. Expansions

Perfectly aware
not a thought
Just the moon
piercing me with light
as I gaze upon it

—Rengetsu / Lotus Moon (1791-1873)

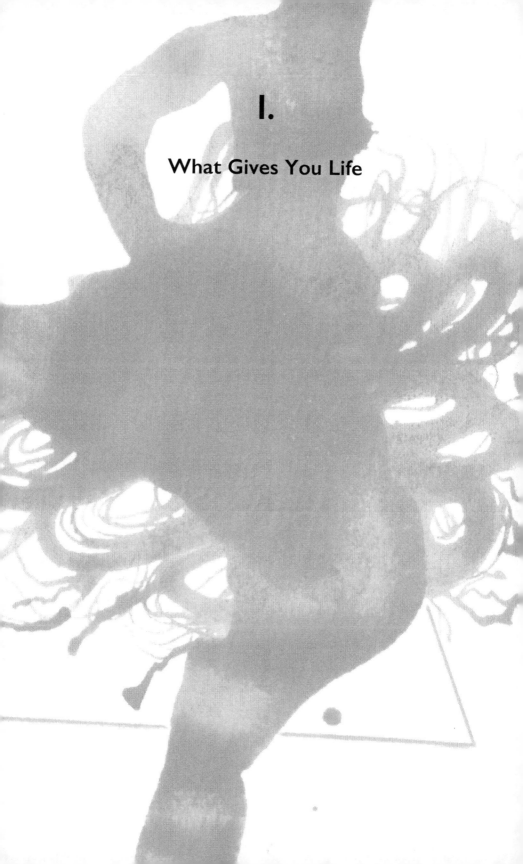

I.

What Gives You Life

Wake Up

Straighten out the
Crest-white smiles
and overlook
expiry dates
for future
Botox fix-me-ups

Ignore the calls for
no fat
no gluten
no fun

Shun hash-tagged
instructions for
how-tos
what-to-dos
if and when the sky falls

Wake up to
what the fuck?

The potential recognition that

this is

y o u r   l i f e

Ignite yourself
invite yourself
to eat up
to devour each breath

to exhale
expel
excrete
the cumbersome
opinions that are
not your own

With this next breath
I invite you
I invite you
to wake up

y o u r l i f e

Alone After Dusk

Just the hum of the hard drive
faint voices outside the window
muffled by tires sliding
on wet night-time asphalt

Click-clacking on the keyboard
hot air escapes the kitchen kettle
sirens in the distance

Alone

with choice

To do
or not to do

The bevy of ever-present
distractions from silence
the inevitable meeting
of oneself

Alone

To feel
or not to feel

An adept ability to
anesthetise in the
doing

Alone

with choice

Be Love

Crawl out from
that claustrophobic prison
within
the fortress of your flesh

Cradle courage
and hear your calling out
primordial prayers
to be understood

Do not shift the
shape of your being or
mold yourself in to another

Honour your wholeness
stay steady
in all that you are
there is nothing in you
that is broken

Work less to be loved
and more to

be love

Begin Again

When there are no words
when the doing isn't working
and the sitting is impossible
when no one wants to
listen anymore to the
sorry tales of what occurred
and how much it hurts

when skins crawls so quickly
it seems to buckle at the joints
and the never-ending stream
of tears lose their salty flavour

when all the facial muscles
fall down below the chin
and bones hang limp
like clothes on the washing line

When there is nothing left
but turning inward and inward
to stroke the weeping
scars of life

we begin again

Bilbo Returns

Crammed cranium
armoured shell
fractured   frail

like the oozing
flesh
of a pink pomegranate
seeds of thinking

spew

     drip

         dominate

devote themselves
to coat soft skin
with sticky stories

Mostly make believe

Clustered clumps
coagulate
create foul forms
apparitions
fuel fear
to writhe its way in

Turning away
feeds the beast

So don't!

Name the wild thing
feed him milk and cookies
and name him Bilbo

He'll like that!
and so will you.

Blissful Imperfection

Sifting through truths
and untruths

Flagrant lies that infest
and infect the make-up
of our minds

Walking

sometimes
running

through the maze of life
to catch
the when-I-this
and the if-I-that

to finally find
that non-existent
perch to
place our perfect arse
and peer down at
the rest of them

Tell me
when you find it!

I've looked in
all the dusty
long-forgotten
corners of my home

I've even ventured out
to search inside *your*
secrets drawers
and walked behind you

to create a facsimile
of *your* reality

I've given up
you see

thrown in the soggy towel
drenched in
blood and sweat

to opt for
front row seats
and watch the sun
come up

and follow it as
it falls away

resting
resting
in blissful imperfection

Blurred Vision

Behind a place we
call
reality
a quiet cavern
full of blurred lines
and untruths

behind the voices
of
integrity

that furtive fumbling
muddled   misguided
make-believe

After years
of courage
and kindness
your dis-ease

a need to numb
to rub out
to turn away from
truth
or to witness the
fairy-tale

a painful dulling
of senses
in an uncomfortable
urgency to un-see
the actuality

To sweep up
the pieces
re-arrange
disagreeable demons
through blurred vision
seeing only purity

Space removes
the vast fictitious veil
eyes wide open
heart still broken
feet turned away

One hand
though   reaching back
to hold onto
to step forward
through the thistles
and the thorns

It is beautiful
on the other side

But Where Do We Go?

When the last crumbs of earth
have sprinkled over our
travel trunks
where the bones lie
and flesh begins to decay—

food for the underground

Where do we go?

Is there a long lighted pathway
with an outstretched hand
or a picnic basket on
a warm summer's day
complete with Grandma's
best cheese scones?

Is there a line up for the
good ones—
an elevator
to hell?
or a parade of virgins
waiting for their
sacrificial grooms to
grab them

So   where do we go?

There are stories
detailed accounts of
the truth
no single story the same

Tell me
is there anyone willing to
go   to stay for days at a time
and return
with Polaroid snap shots
of their holiday
in the afterlife?

Tell me   where do we go?

Calm

Curious

It seems today there are
no words
no stream of thoughts
no offshoots
or meanderings
no pondering the past

Mystified
when pen touches paper

nothing

except perhaps
the *why* or *where*
they might have escaped to

a faint fluttering
of future sends
a soft quiver through each cell
a sort of quiet anticipation

Carnal Caressing

When swelling anticipation
precedes
the subtle hum
of awakening
and arousal

an invitation
a traveling

that downward dancing
a carnal caressing
of each and every vertebra
where Eros ignites
bursts and births
liquid lava—
an expansion
feeding into molecules
or thick hot honey
seeping into
flesh   ripe
a pooling
a pulsing-into
quivering pelvic bones

A writhing
an undulation
a seductive cellular weaving
skin stroking skin—

then   silence
where that sensory seeking
subsides
it dissolves into divinity

and where mortality is secondary
separation slips away

and the pause is eternity
where loves Love fingers
stroke serenity

a momentary godliness
of touch

Celestial Faerie Dust

In the seeking of reality
I am struck by the banality
of ever present questions
to life's uncertain circumstance

The more why what and when
that plagues the space
between the ears

The drive to awaken
find the truth
save us from our fears

Who has the answers?
Who holds the
magic manifesto
that waves the wand
of wisdom?

Where celestial faerie dust
like witchcraft
wipes away
wishy-washy thinking
to tempt our trust

Is it invisible?
or sitting in our cells?

Can the cloaked bald man
with upright spine
unlock the definitive truth?

Or is the wooden statue
blood dripping from
its palms my guide
to certain serenity?

In the space between the ears
we seek the truth
to save us from our fears

Cellular Creases

Hold out those hands
and cup them

cup them to
cradle the left inside the right

and soften
to hold the hurt
and honour its existence

Trust that in turning away
the memories of yesterday
merely nestle themselves
in to your cellular creases

Only to crawl out again
in the mirror of
your daily life

Just as worthy as your
greatest achievements
your hurt needs your attention
your kindness and your patience

Tread with tenderness
hold your hurt
to recognize when and how
you can help another

Your Chubby Little Fingers

When was the moment
that your chubby
little fingers let go of
wanting to touch
wonder?

When was it that
you weren't so
sure anymore
if your makers
knew everything?

What happened
to stop you from
seeing benevolent
beauty in your
mother's eyes?

Do you remember?

Was there a moment
in time
ingrained in your
being when
you started to
clothe yourself
in armour?

Or was it more
a gradual layering
a caking-on

coating
muddy memories
that hardened over time
protecting you from

possible
probable
pain?

Have you yet
peered into the
eyes of strangers
quietly comparing
their faery tale
to yours?

What would you
surrender
to reawaken wonder?

How much are you willing to lose?

Closer to 50

No more longing
for yesterdays
not all those questions
nor numerous
definitive answers rendered then

No rushing into tomorrows
to find the when I this and that
no coveting of smooth skin
nor sex appeal

Instead
just lingering
in this lust for life
basking in the now-nebulous-
no-ground
the knowing of nothing to be
true

These hopeful musings that
this is not everything

the humour
in my very own
human-ness
and
perhaps
the hope for humility

just to touch it

Coming Home

Mere seconds after
that first *hello*
quiet curiosity catches
my attention

coaxing me to step
a little closer
to soak up your scent
and investigate
soft crevasses
cradling the corners
of your lips

You smile

wide open
as if
somehow
we have met before

and known each others
secrets   sat beneath
a thousand willow trees

Silently
remembering
lifetimes ago

And when
the webbing of your
fingers folds into mine
there's a pulsing that
loops and loops

Like the longing
for a song to never end

where crescendo
and quiet coexist

and intermingle

Cracked Open

On this day
when no one else was looking
you peered down
stared   in fact
to watch the layers
of a hardened past

The untruths
begin to slip off
drip off
dissolve into ground

On this day
there was less of you
to hide

The Dewy Wound

Where a heart beats
muffled
to hide
the hurt
beneath
a dewy wound
wrapped neatly
inside
the pretty package
of smiles and niceties

Where the busy mind
winds through webs of
what-ifs and why-nots
and even the
why do I care?

When
allowing tears
to tumble
becomes
the humble gift
of gratitude
for long forgotten
feelings

and the not-knowing
is the birthplace
of freedom
from shackles of shame
from the paralysis
of poisoned perception

where there is
nothing left but
empty space
to quietly touch
and caress
the hurting in the heart

Dip Your Toe Back In

Revisiting what once was
after sitting with what is
becomes a curious
experience with oneself

Perceptions from the past
mired by stories
from long before
can start to slip away

Dipping your toe back
     in
        and out
and   in
        and out

Cautious
yet
somehow   not afraid

Resolutions
to still the mind
to stay steady
to step forward
slowly   sublimely
without suspicion

Promise
to listen deeply
to accept
absolutely
the unbridled unfolding
of today's reality
and tomorrow's

yet to be revealed

Do What Gives You Life

When there are only questions

When the jaw cracks open
offering only twisted syllables
tripping and tumbling
over your tongue

When the only answer
is to sit in silence—
in crowded solitude
to quieten the toe-tapping
in your mind

Drop down
drop down to the
pit of your Buddha-belly—
the seat of your soul

To listen

to listen
with divine patience
and feel the pin driving
that ignition
to kinaesthetic connection

New hallowed knowledge

that travels through the
flesh of your being
to break the chains of confusion
and set your sacred spirit free

II.

Through the Wilderness

Masturbation of the Mind

F *alse*
E *vidence*
A *ppearing*
R *eal*

Is there no
escape
from the
tick-tocking
brain-rocking
masturbation
of the mind

Where is relief
from the thirsty
craving to
fill up
stuff down
lacerate the soul

Why the need
to imbibe the
crazed *Koolaid*
the lure of
insanity

Truth shall set you free

In the pause
to attend
to comfort the beast
that drains the physical
plumbing

Pump air through
first-rate filtration systems

Rewire out-dated
circuits

Painstaking
provocative

A prerequisite
for
survival
of the fittest

Filo Pastry

Paper-thin skin
like flakey filo pastry
coats the corporal hollowness

Behold!

A cavern
not dark
nor fearful

Instead a sort of
nothingness

silent
but not
Still

No breath
no noise
no voice

Puncture your periphery
to hear the
hissing hollowness
seep its way
into your surroundings
your life circumstance

More and more
become aware
and mindful not to stare
at your reflection

For Fuck's Sake

When you arrived
they told you
you were broken
needed to surrender
step over to the
winning side

Through your
blurry eyes
you weren't quite
ready to believe them

Your bones were brittle
you barely
sensed your skin
yet you did not
feel broken

For fuck's sake!

You had made it this far
flourished
using foolproof tools
to survive
the story of your life

They looked at you
like Pollyanna peering
through her rose-coloured
spectacles

You were tired
agreed to take a seat
and listen in

Yet   a life time of
invaluable selfless
suggestions to
others
deafened you

It would take
countless days
thousands in fact

Until you could hear
until you could heal
into your wholeness

Fuck It!

When the world turns—
flares its hairy nostrils
and snarls back at you

When   no matter where
you look
there's no way out

and the only possible
answer appears
MAGIC!

Immediate relief—
release from
rigid responsibility
from remorse for what was
and respite from what will be

That moment arrives
that *fuck it* moment
the—*I don't give a shit*
the—*I can't stand to sit*
in the stench of my own
sweaty skin

Unwilling   unready
exhausted by any effort
even thinking is too much

Poor me
poor me
pour me a fucking drink!

Gaze Over Your Shoulder

Oh   the places you've been
this wild and wondrous
one-day-at-a-time

As you turn your feet away
remember
remember all the beauty

The way your heart
cracked open because
you *finally* gave it permission

As you turn this corner
gently gaze over your shoulder
to recall

the choices
that led
to your today

Regret not a thing

Instead   Sweet One
embrace
embrace each sacred second
of today

and know
know you are not
alone

ever

How Fast Does the Earth Spin?

600 miles an hour …

She thought
she could

Catch it!

What if?
she stopped

Just paused

Pretended
she was

Already dead

She might

Feel

The touch of a hand

She might

Notice

That soft pink
skin on his forgotten finger

She might

Hear

Words clearly
without her armchair quarterback

She might
be

Fully Present

What if
She knew

Silence is enough

Hungry

Quickened cadence
courts the heart

Catch your breath
to hold it

Pay attention
to rivers of blood

Pulsing through
humid lips

darting down
thirsty tongue

trembling

Flooding the voracious
vessel of your being

Cells stimulate
sensory stirring

Press up against
each other

Begin

In the Wilderness Again

In the wilderness again
ten years after
slipping off my steel-toed stilettos

Tentative

Ready to spread my toes
on an unfamiliar road
and step forward

Looking for the ground again
to press my feet into

There is no path back

I have looked over my shoulder
a thousand times
to check

There is comfort in closing eyes
to turn against the wind
and fall backwards
into faith

To spread my softened wings

Trusting

The path will reveal itself
in flight

Intoxication

As if faerie dust had
bathed the ground tonight
even the moon softened
offering privacy

and the fleshy grass nestled
its way into the small of your back
the curve of your neck
caressing your limbs each time
your rhythm changed

Intoxication

Now and then
when the damp breeze
touched your lips
it made you quiver
and quickened the cadence
of your heart

The Ground

Feel the ground
come up and kiss your feet

As you stand to attention
primped and starched
ready for inspection

Be willing
willing to allow
the matrix of your
liquid-crystal self
to hear

the call to surrender

To surrender that
excruciating effort

That once-upon-a-time
served you well

a sword and shield
against that never-ending
cluster bombing

the way you saw your life

this craft you learned
long long ago
to keep your weapons close
and guard yourself

Awake   alert your adversary
to your very own life

until that effort became
a rancid recipe to suit up
and show up in your

crisp white shirt
polished shoes
polished smile
all so shiny

The walking dead

thick blood
like molasses drained
from every vein

Muscles limply
hanging off bone

Breath so shallow
only a whimper
to finally ask for

help

So so simple

Sword and shield drop
your opponents run
towards you

scoop up your bony
fragile figure

help you to surrender
and carry you to the other side

Where there is strength in numbers
and the fellowship of the spirit
seeks only to soothe and heal
the scrapes and splinters of your life

You feel your feet on the ground
and now know

there is no one left
to fight

Until We Meet Again

Sunlight stretches its fingers
through Venetian blinds
making miniature dust particles
dance

Children play outside
and in the distance
a train warns of its
imminent arrival

Once crisp white sheets
now rumpled
warm with memories
of last night

You
asleep   dew on your brow
purring
cradling blankets
close to you

I consider stirring you
consider caressing your
silver temples
press my lips to
the curve of your neck

A quiet pause
preparing
to make myself invisible
not challenging
the state of inertia

One last look

You
stir
and I

disappear

until
we
meet
again

Living Lexicon

Burrow through
the webbing of your skin
though the tissues
that hold together the very
scaffolding of your being

Enter your
celestial centre

It is here   Sweet One
you will find
what you are seeking
invisible to the human eye
untouchable to the hand

Yet you know
somehow   you already know
it is here

Every answer to
every question
woven into your very own
living lexicon

Perhaps
you have been here before
learned lessons
from countless other crusades
drawing you closer
and closer
to enlightenment

and perhaps
this is *it*

Perhaps you just came
with an untouchable
invisible instruction manual

one that only you
can feel

Be still   Sweet One
to unravel your questions
uncover your answers
laid out in your
living lexicon

Looking at the Moon

Alone
cocooned in my room
closing my eyes
soothed by
harmonious humming
the world outside
over my shoulder
Your side of the bed
unruffled

An empty guitar case
leans lifeless
against cream coloured walls

Those silly little bells
wait for your
mischievous ringing
Your ritual
bringing each session
to order

Through the dusty blinds
the moon appears and dissolves
behind windblown branches

A breeze kisses my cheeks
I wonder if you
are looking at the moon

III.

Midlife

Midlife

In the beginning

you were not consulted
on your ETA
your arrival
to this earth

you just arrived
one fine day
probably shocked
when the frosty breeze
tickled the surface of
your skin

Until   of course
they swaddled you
and gave you
to your mother

You couldn't quite make
out the features in her face
or the color of her eyes

but you didn't mind
She was all yours
She was all love

She and others
showed you
how and
who to be

You watched and learned

created your own
perceptions of
peculiarities
and perplexities of
your own existence

You became the owner
of this person you created
in your mind

Year after year
you made decisions
based on stories you heard
and ones you created
until they became
solid truth
the only truth

until you realized
there is

No solid ground

It happens to the best of us!

Sometimes in
a split second
sometimes dragging on
for years

little whispers of
maybes and possiblys

And what if I am wrong?

You sat in disbelief

Questions
so many questions

Where to begin
on this glorious quest
for more answers
more truths

To possibly be proven wrong

yet again …

Mindfuck

Thoughts creep in
like old growth

Knotted branches
tangled and twisted
grow into each other

a myriad of made-up
mind mush
make-believe mumblings
seep into cranial crevices
virus-like

The voice
starving to projectile vomit
irrational idiotic ideas
just to free the body
of their choke-hold

They trip and tumble off
the tongue   clumsily
scraping over parched
taste buds

A mi-nute momentary
minute of purity
a purging of poison
and then a listening

Where words surge back in
chasing each other
with dexterity down
never-ending
ear canals

Crashing and colliding
bombarding the body
for a second time

My Breathing Bones

Skin softened
muscles slipping
away from bone

Bone—
        so supple
it breathes

Open

Open to
my humanness

I choose

I choose to
unpack   unravel   undo

undress down to
my breathing bones

And then
I choose to rest
to drape a veil over
the tissues that are my body
until I am ready again

There is no piecing back
together of the jagged shards

It is too late to close my eyes

Oh heavens
how I have tried

I have tried to
wrap myself in
pretence and perfection

but these breathing bones
cast aside my efforts
like a disinterested lover

I am open
to my humanness

Naked

When just below the
bellybutton
the flip-flopping and the
whoosh wakes up
and the touch of a hand
across a restaurant table
sends goose bumps
down my spine   I go
on an all encompassing
joy ride

When the skin's surface
craves contact
and the deep wells
of the eyes
ignite both
stillness and desire

When there's no choice
anymore
but to peel away
each layer

You stand
fully naked
silver stretch marks
and all

When there's no wanting
to cover up
clamp down
clear out or
control

When all is quiet
and content

You say
it is in the night-time
when my eyes open wide
wider than by day

Yet
it is only in the confines
of our cocoon
when the world sleeps
and we lie awake
with no words
naked
encased
engulfed

When pulsing pupils
serve to fructify
lay fertile ground
to expose
to yoke

It is your gaze
that lovingly
creates
a refuge
to reveal
your radiant
reflection
in my eyes

No Reprieve

Each

  new day

   begging

    for pain

     to

      please

       go away

       and

       yet

        no reprieve

               It firmly persists
               permeates every cell
               purposely presses
               crushes chest bones
               melts flesh

               tears
               stream

            down

          chaffed

         cheeks

Gulping air
to catch breath

                                        wherever

                            whenever

                    possible

No shields left
to hold against the heart

No more bricks to
build barriers

No bootstraps
to pull up

Just tears
tumbling

        down

                chaffed

                        cheeks

Until

there are no more

Until

there are no more left

No Tears for Dying

No real tears yet
I wish they would
breach the banks
of the eyes
weigh down each
lash
and bleach pathways
through bronzed skin

It's as if
they've all retreated
conjoined
and nestled neatly
on the diaphragm's dome
constricting breath
allowing only inhalation—

a centaur's sword
threatening my own
death
with even-thoughts
of breath

Memories
wash over glazed eyeballs

Only the good ones
for now
as if the little me
lived a fairy-tale

Flashback of gumboots
and vast open spaces
of that naughty smile
the one I inherited

Heaving breath in
blowing breath out

Waiting

waiting for tears of dying

Not Looking

Not looking I saw something
not grasping I touched something

Or did it touch me?

No boundaries make it hard to tell

At first a pin prick of light
from deep behind the balls of my eyes
then a black cloud
washes away the brightness

A flutter of excitement
and all is quiet

Back to breath and emptiness

Again the light appears
bursting this time
warming the insides of my lids
trickling down my throat like honey
until it reaches the centre of my very being

A surge   two giant loving hands
push from inside my ribcage
forcing the crown of my head skywards
and roots to sprout from my lower limbs

And then again
a snap of the mind
I am back

Nothing will ever be the same

On the Precipice

Standing on the precipice
with the breeze behind your back
A teetering-tottering of trust

That tremendously tall T-word
that tinkers with the should-I
and flits with the should-I-nots

Standing on the tips
of your toes to peer
over the perimeter

gauging the possible pain
the scrapes and splinters
yet knowing too the potential

that the wind might carry you
cradle you   in fact
teach you the *truth*

about Trust
that very tall T-word

that dissection of dialogue
destroys the very
essence of the now

holds you back in
the yesterday and
suffocates today

Peel Away

In the peeling back
of
years
of
shields and armour
now visible to the
discerning
naked eye
the crusty remains
of battle scars
old weeping stories
old beliefs

Past attempts made
to
re-bandage
to
mummify old memories
yet underneath
gaping wounds remain

Weak and not yet healed
they are tender to touch
even the light
can agitate the fleshy fibres
and cause discomfort

Thorough
empathetic examination
cathartic cleansing
beneath the lacerations
of the heart
exposed

A re-weaving of
fissures and fibres
bumpy and bruised
courting circulation

re-growth

to awaken

to re-awaken

Pillow Talk

All curled up
face to face caressing
the road map of your life
you are my marked mirror

One ear nestled
the other open
just to listen

Lashes heavy
not weighed down
just allowing
both eyes
to see clearly
to be seen

Where the answers are
where the strings
of your soul
sweep over my cells
and delve deep
inside of me

A sort of
symbiotic safety
a place of heart-healing
where there is no
wanting   no needing

Just a loud hush
in transformation

Close Your Eyes

Quiet ...

so very quiet

Subtle
pulsing on
the surface of
your skin

Close your tired eyes

Close them
to see more clearly
to peer inside

Where all the answers
wait so patiently

for you
to find them

in your own time

Rajasic Nonsense

That busy little mind
all bunched up with
mis-matched mis-sized
prickly musings that
make no sense

Those knee-jerk reactions
those decisions
those actions to let go
and grab hold of
what to do right now

The presence

The-paying-attention-to-the-wants
and the no-nonsense-needs of loved ones

The possibility of pause
where the line between
yes and no
molds itself in to
the sphere of choice

where the busy little mind
momentarily shuts down
suspends thinking

trusting what is

Rejoice!

Finally

tears

First hiding furtively
inside the umbrellas of your eyes

Soon enough though
they rejoice

burgeon

basking in their
courageous
cascading

creating their very
own tributaries
tumbling
hurried
they weave
working their way
into
well-like wrinkles

Falling
they free themselves from
your fragile face
until
they settle

they settle
coaxed into crevices
behind the collar bone—

Until
of course

again

they arrive

Sometimes
when you're quiet
searching for nothing
not looking for the
next new way
to feel better
be braver
unravel the world's mysteries
the obstacles
that were there
yesterday
vanish
like they
were never there
at all
overjoyed
you stretch out your fingers
to touch
nothing
breathless
only for a moment
for in the reaching
to grasp nothing
something
reappears

Vacuous

The mind finally quiet
just for a breath   Relief

Sit

again
upright yet relaxed

Wait

for something
anything

Observe

tantric dances
in the mind

Come back

over and over
come back

Look

look behind
the closed eyelids

See

see yourself truly
you are beautiful

Escape from Shame

Calloused crusted layers
of shame
petrified
the stories of your life

Fortress-like dams
thwarted all attempts
to cleanse your shattered soul
through unrestricted tears

Machinations of the mind
conjured up
constant commentary
convincing you
you are / were not enough

There was a time
        Remember?
when your own perception
was a prison
padlocked by your own hand

And *remember* when

You turned toward
that tiny pinhole of light
enough to see the shadow
the one you resided in
the one you could not stand

*

Ready now to unfold

Unravelling the years of unseeing
wrapped and bound by
your very being

Willing
willing to show yourself

Show yourself in all
your naked humanness

to write a new story
and begin again

Shards of Shame

In the searching
through your heavy bag
of go-to tools
the ones you use
to fend of
fictitious
fanciful foes

Let's just call them   f e a r

You scrape your fingers
are bitten by broken pieces
shattered shards
of shame

Shocked
you tear open
your bag
peer deep inside
to look for more

There is plenty

Like a mold
growing on fermenting fruit
the piece you left
for years
crouching quietly
at the back of your
refrigerator

You know you cannot
leave it here

It will only multiply
grow and fuse together
seep through the canvas
of your bag

start to spread itself
through sickly cells
then infect the very
structure of your-
self

Diligently
piece by piece
you pick out
prickly profuse
possessions

your bag
crawling with
this cancer

nauseating nonsensical
knowledge

a necessary cleansing
to make space

to replace
this space
with

nothing

IV.

In the Space of Solitude

mind mumblings
slowly cease
possibility
for
pause
and
reflection
on
right and wrong
on
wants and needs
on
then and there
and
now
and
in the time
between
a shifting
a changing
a rearranging
where discomfort births
some ease
no someone or something
to fill the gaps
complete the picture
to fix or change
what's here
a remembering again today
how beautiful we are
and that
alone
we are
enough

Stay Where Your Hands Are

Remembering
yesterdays
when
everything
was
perfect

Contemplating
tomorrows
where
the what-ifs
and the Oh-My-Gods
breed
bloodthirsty
beasts

Coaxing
consciousness
back to where
the hands are

Surrender

The body's fortress
now so secure
each crack and fissure
diligently
filled   fused   reinforced

to intercept
to thwart
unwanted visitors
invaders

Your story

Lessons learned
from life's lashings

Scars
hastily healed
left you
licking your wounds

Vigilant
and on duty
day after day
no rest for the weary

Please—

Sweet child
so spent from
your struggle

Surrender!
Surrender and
invite your
imagined adversaries
inside

They are not
separate from you

You are your only
enemy

You and
your mind

That's It!

As you trudge
destiny's happy road

to sure and certain serenity
to real raw recovery
a sudden moment of clarity!

Jubilation and Revelation!

That's it!

It was yesterday
you woke
sleep stuck
between your lids

A single word

the answer
to *all* the questions
was bouncing
through your hectic brain

G r a t i t u d e !

That's it!

So you work and
weave it into your life
with confidence

No more mishaps
because you found
that magical propriety

In fact
invented it with
your own fine-tuned
perceptions

Poof!

All your problems
vanish
your life is
like a dream

You now realize
this is what you
hadn't seen!

and yet

as time slips by
and the days multiply—

G r a t i t u d e

is not enough …

Still seeking the antidote
to cast out doubt and fear

Another day
a new
Aha! will
suddenly appear

Perhaps it's patience
without the pride
or service and surrender

You'll have another
and another
magnificent idea

Until one day
you'll remember

no promises

That's it!

The Chains of Despair

Unwind the chains

the ones you bound
yourself with

free your fragile self
from the noose of despair

The ones that
lacerate your flesh
cut the vital nourishment
from your soul

Expose the fresh wounds

First—to yourself
then—to another

Breathe new life
into your every cell

Bear witness to your
mighty vulnerability

Drop the grave weight
of wanting

Be still and see
what has always been there

You are beautiful

Through the Forest

Sweep away
the twisted brambles
even as they spring back
and scrape the skin
off your face

Take larger steps than you
imagined possible

Climb crooked rocks

    and

sink sentient slippers
into the earth

Stay steady
traversing nebulous
un-trodden terrain

    and

    pause

pause
in the possibility

Seek to see more clearly

    and

close your eyes

coaxing lashes
to briefly

      kiss

fluid-crystal breath
pulsing through your being

To let
wing-like lungs
hold your whole heart

The Glass Slipper

Stories
we all love stories

fluffy little faerie tales
fantasies of what it
could and should be like

Surely there's
a glass slipper
waiting for each of us

a happily-ever-after

Cross each ' t ' and
dot each ' i '
blot out the blemishes
of life's battles

Create a perfect picture
a little lip gloss
a nip
a tuck

Good to go!

Trouble is
when the sun's a little hotter
and beads of perspiration
begin to form
on your forehead
we'll see the fine creases
the groves
the crevasses

When you've licked your lips
greedy for the last drops of

your green smoothie

and the corners of your mouth
hold remnants of your mousy meal

When there no money to
touch up last year's botox

And your secret midnight scoffings
of oh-so-good
organic ice cream
creep up around your waistline

You'll just be left with you

a little crumply in places
some sharp edges
where you'd hoped
for sultry angles

No more thigh gap

The Spaces in Between

Where the ground disappears
so too that delusional delineation
between self and all else

where the mind dissolves
and breath steps in

      effortlessly

Where the hole in the soul
stops seeking for food
to sustain cellular memories
long long idle

Fleeting but visible
moments of nothingness
lost only to
fruitless grasping
for more

When the grip
slips

      surrenders

falling
falling back into
the space in between
where the ground disappears
and the breath steps in

      effortlessly

That Voice

Gnawing   grinding   parasitic
that visceral voice
silently scurrying through
veins
through arteries
with direct intent

Once settled
it makes its nest
scratching away entire cells

It sits there
proud   defiant
confident it belongs there
anxiously feeding off human flesh

It guards its ground
thoroughly convincing—
practiced
skilled
praying on ego

It cannot and *will* not be
forced out

Like a feral beast
who might be tamed
its only adversary
is tenderness

A patient waiting
an honest wanting-
to-befriend   to behold
to attend

to allow
a way out through
bone and skin

A dissolving-into
empty ground

A space evacuated

available for new
visitors
kept open
just in case

The Want Monster

When more is not enough

When
malformations of the mind
snatch and seize
the wants
the ifs
the whens

When more is not enough

Gratitude for haves and have-nots
grasp instead
for greedy cravings
to comfort
loneliness and lacking

When more is not enough

Where quiet
is confinement
and
ravenous rajasic appetites
emerge

Wet frothy lips

When more is not enough

The Wind Picks Up

Alone
        Dust settled
                Quiet

Without warning
a warm
wistful breeze slips in

First just a faint
whisper

picking up
puny perceptions
from the past

        A stirring

As the wind seizes
the scent of the
almost forgotten
flashing back

full force

Not just flickering
memories anymore

Full flesh and blood
feelings
pulsing
permeating

        This cellular heart beat

Through the Goo

From the cauldron
of the belly
where Agni ignites
agitates and aggravates
both desire and digestion

In this 800 millionth life
we get to choose
the form of that fire

From the flesh and bones
Through the tissues of the goo
To the very essence of humanity
where the Atman sits
cradled by the humming heart

Do we feed the hungry beast
with narcissistic nourishment
or caress each cell with
selfless service
seeking nothing but
the purest perception
of Purusha?

In this universal
creation of consciousness
where we bear the generous gift
of divine discernment
we get to choose
to de-cide which side
to kill with burning desire
to train the Tapas
to teach us

To teach us
the answers in this
university called life

Tributaries

Those crevasses
that flank the corners
of your eyes
are not wounds
from wars
waged in this lifetime

They are not
merely signs
of your immortality

Trust instead
that they are
tributaries
leading your loved ones

Inviting others
to witness the window
into your wholeness—honestly—

Tumbleweed

Wandering
lost in the desert of your life
like rolling tumble weed
skipping along
the edges of the road
holding on to heavy debris
and the wind keeps blowing
tossing you forward
sometimes trapping you
in a corner
for days and days

Until with no warning
the winds change
and nudge you
unfix you from your stalemate

You collide with other
tangled branches
weaving yourselves together

Squirming
you wait for the next gust
to unglue you   to unravel you

Free to roll on
unleash your debris
buoyant
you frolic into open fields
kiss the carpet of
moist rich grass
stretch yourself out
to bask in the
fragrant
strawberry canyon

Turquoise Lake

Peripheral vision
and perked up ears
feed your hyper-vigilance

Alert
on my behalf
the wide berth of your back
carries my weight
permitting me to feign
fearlessness

As you trot us forward
holding back a canter

Do I dare to whisper
I am afraid?

There   I've said it!

It is in the telling
of the truth
that I can cup
a few precious drops
of courage

before they slip
through the gaps
between my fingers

Past attempts to grasp and grapple
greedily
on to fearlessness
have indeed been futile

You are steady

Even as your flesh
feels my fearful heartbeat

and you pause
to look just ahead

into the stillness of
the turquoise lake

February 28, 2016

Twisted Tongues

Tripping over twisted tongues
transformation comes

with tricky little twists and turns and
traps that catch you when you think

you've got it—
but you don't!

Single-handed
you thought you climbed

that mountain
thought you'd found

your lotus flower
but you didn't—

not just yet!
Awake and open

you sit up
suit up

put on your big girl panties
make them notice

you this time—
but they don't!

Then   remember one fine day
to listen intently

slow down to a halt
notice who you are

what you do
and why you do it

Perhaps there's hope for you yet!

Until They Come Again

Pause to ponder
what is true and
which core
convictions serve only
to suffocate   to starve

Pause to find
the subtle separation
between pre-pubescent programming
and mindful meditation

Response vs. reaction
comfort in dis-ease
painfully peering backward
dragging sacksful of
slop and swill
to piece together savvy solutions

Instead
relinquish tight-fisted clutching
witness and befriend
fabrications of the mind
invite them to be seen
observe   attend   wait

until they come again

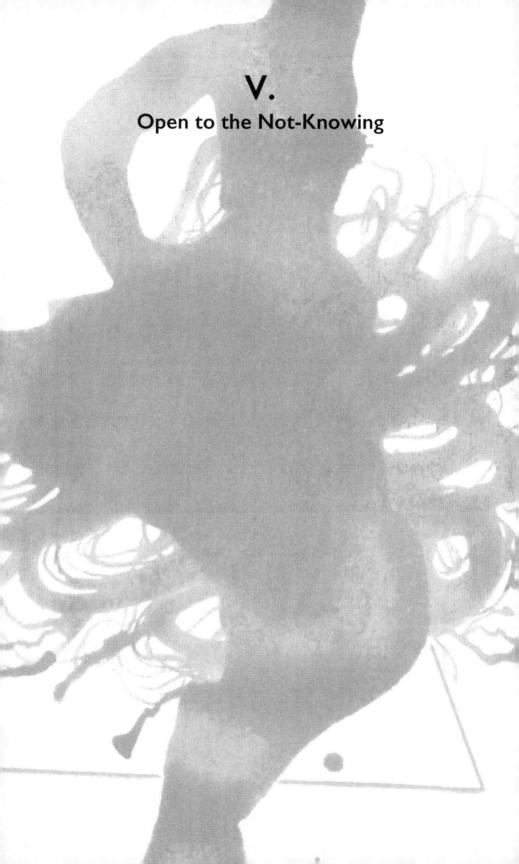

V.
Open to the Not-Knowing

Upon Awakening

Behind busy eyelids
mind begins its daily dance—

its pestering
to perpetuate stories from the past—

begins its tenacious ticktock
its prodding with tomorrow's to-do-list

Body rolls—heaves itself
feet planted on the Earth

Skin shivers as breath enters slowly
and heart is invited to pulse a little faster

And just like yesterday   knees buckle
to rest on well worn-woollen ground

Palms cup cranium as
elbows burrow into bed

                  Where the day begins …

a re-wiring   re-setting
a remembering-who-I-am

a simple conversation
with a wise world

Wag the Finger

Go ahead!

Wag the finger
like a weapon
of blame

all the shoulds
and should-nots
all the somebodys

Who clearly caused
that dreadful discomfort
in your life

Close your eyes
Shut them tight!
to the stark reflection

the illusion of blind innocence

Each day
paint on the stiff
stony armour

and stand in the knowing
that your are *right*
and that you deserve more

Feed it!
feed yourself with
whatever you find

to fill up and foster
your earned
entitlement

Pray   there will come a day
maybe tomorrow
when the frantic filling up

With *anything*
and the unrelenting urge
to be right will slip away

when the veils
of desperate deception
will dissolve

and the palms of the hands
will open
to the not-knowing

Waiting for Words

Fingers poised
on plastic pegs

Ready
to receive
their wisdom

Curious how
this Magic Machine
stores so much

Internal
information

Each digit quivering
for a sign   a signal
a touching into truth

Waiting
Waiting

for feckless
letters to unravel
to unfold ripe with guidance

Tonight   though
Nothing

A vain silence
and fingers stiffen
in a relative rigor mortis

Left wanting
like a taunted toddler

With empty promises
of vanilla ice cream

A silent chuckle   stirs
a message from Microsoft
ready to emerge:

CTL + ALT + DEL

Waiting

                So still

pulsing heart

perceivable on

blood-filled lips

                So still

sensing hair breathe

through skin—blades

of grass seeking sunlight

                So still

Sounds and smells

from yesterday

seep into each nostril

                caressing   coaxing   memories

                Now   waiting

Lungs   cradling   holding   heart-space

                *

That gentle tugging of time

trying to turn a little quicker

To touch

The tips
of
my
fingers

traverse
the creases
and crevasses

of your face

What When How Where Why

What *is* really good enough?

What *is* the elusive equation
for wholeness?

When do we lose sight of that
once-potent ever-present
preoccupation with pure joy?

On what day do we recognize
our brokenness?

—and begin to piece together
sharp fragments?

Those gaping holes between
the pieces ...

How do we courageously
court curious investigation?

—the space between
the broken shards?

Where do we begin? And why?

When It's Time

When it's time
and only then
        tiny fissures
                breathe into
                        tributaries and flood
                                cells with long

                                buried
long
calcified
razor-sharp
                memories and emotions
                        yearning   begging to escape

When it's time
and the brain can no

longer   trap   and

                hold onto toxic untruths
                        it begins to burst its way

through the confines
of the heavily guarded cranium

When it's time
and only then
                        the stoic soldier
                        surrenders the shield
                        surrenders the story to

        v   a   s   t   o   p   e   n   s   p   a   c   e

When the Past Slides In

When the past slides in the back door

unannounced   silent   stealthily

it ignites a practical
                    pinball effect

Stories   long stuffed away
burst into consciousness

When the past slides in without warning

Wantings and wishings
create copious counterfeit memories

filling each cell
with fraudulent flashbacks

flooding the body
with chemicals

When the past slides in ...

Halt
     to find ground

Retaliate politely against
deceptive deductions—and

just smile

When the Winds Change

It is a little startling when the winds change
as if they've never shifted course before

We stop to wonder why
even wait to make sure
we are not mistaken

And yet they *do* change
over and over again

They do not ask our permission
or prepare us for uncertainty

They just take a deep breath in
and blow the other way

We re-adjust we re-define
we remember how to walk
on uneven ground

even let ourselves be blown about
colliding into prickly places

and in the plucking-out of the thorns
the picking up of ourselves

A certain courage is needed
to walk with winds
as they hold us up—

until
        they change
                yet again

Where the Wild Things Are

It must be so
I can't be   wrong
I've thought about it for too long
inside my head

There are these creatures
that act like barbaric leeches
sucking up the empty space
leaving not a single trace

                    of sanity

> *(Yet even as I sit*
> *to write this rather*
> *convoluted ditty*
> *I must admit*
> *I've asked myself*
> *if these thoughts*
> *are more than shitty)*

I wonder if I just

                    shut up

would the creatures
just go away
my guess is no
I'm not that lucky

They'd just come back

                    another day!

Wild and Wondrous

Oh the places you've been

    This wild and wondrous

one-day-at-a-time

    As you turn your feet away

remember the beauty

    and the way your heart

cracked open

    because

you finally gave it permission

As you gently turn this corner

    gaze over your shoulder

to recall

    recall the decisions that lead

to your today

    regret not one

not one thing

You Remembered

On this day
when no one else was looking
you peered down
stared
to watch the layers
of hardened past
the untruths
begin to slip
then drip right off
and dissolve into the earth

On this day
there was less of you
less of you
to hide
and in your nakedness
you felt cradled by
your own arms

They had been there
all along
only invisible to you
until—

on this day
you remembered
you remembered you were nothing
and

you were everything

Your Mother's Womb

A long time ago
before you could speak or see
before you knew your name
you were an amphibian
floating   cocooned in
your mother's warm womb

You learned your first instrument
felt it pulse through your cells

Your mother was your teacher
as you patiently waited
for your turn on Earth
her heartbeat rocked you to sleep
told you: *you are safe*
yoked you to her   forever

Taught you
you are connected to

everyone   everything

Sometimes you forget

So   be still
and close your eyes
to remember

Send Help

Frantic   frenzied   fighting God

figuring   fumbling   feeling future surfing

writhing   seething

Knowing nothing   not believing

wanting   needing   and perceiving

others' actions   as deceiving

Fortune telling   teardrops welling

Pride and ego   chest is swelling

K   A   B   O   O   M

No Control   hit the ground

Lose   your   soul

Damming   demonistic dive

Stretch   your   hand   out

S   U   R   V   I   V   E

Cocoon

Our cocoon…

that protective layer of our
own virtual reality

Harvested habits
sticky software of the mind

Torturous two A.M. tactics
for tomorrow's tasks
seem tremendous at the time

Mulling over morality
avoiding our own reality

Oh to be so right!

The persistent pressure
to have the all the answers

To offer altruistic advice
and know it *all*

So that we are good enough

To peel away the cocoon
is to open to the possibility

To rest back and relax
in the groundlessness
of not-knowing

Instructions to meditate

Invitation to sit on
the groundless ground
connecting the body to
an imaginary solidity

Invitation to

Stay here
anchored to waves of breath
Easily accessible
deep in the bowl of the belly

Where

expansion into presence
yawns in all four directions

Sweet tender moment
and then
a tender touching of thoughts
turns into
provocative future fantasies
and paralyzing play-by-plays
for the past

The elusive present moment

Ah yes ... t h e   b r e a t h !

To begin again

What If You Are Not Broken?

Meander through the old growth
to marvel at this misshapen
deciduous majesty

Standing steady
far beyond your vision

Step closer to touch
caress the gnarled
wounds earned
from just standing here

From standing here
and swaying in the wind

How wondrous!
How beautiful!

These courageous soldiers
rooted to our earth

Breathing machines
allowing life to
move through them ...

What if *you* are not broken?

What if you stepped closer
to your wounds
and caressed them?

Accepting
Allowing

Marvelling at
the miracle of life
moving through you

VI.
The Elephant in the Room

The Elephant in the Room

Shh…

Don't say a word
steer your gaze
away from the very large
creature standing smack
in the middle of your life

Tiptoe around

Don't disturb the beast

Consider cupping your ears
to muffle the
intermittent trumpet calls

To   look at me

And   in your looking-away
the creature grows
and grows

A giant *wild* animal
lurking in your living room

It's trunk so large
at times you notice
shards of bone china
lying on the ground

A quick kick to the corner
a fluffing up of furniture

There   It's all *good!*

Sneaky little

critters **creeping** into

mental **machinery** messing

with **the mind** bring mischievous

monkeys **swinging** on virtual vines

creating **havoc** inside your already crowded

cranium looping **manmade** myths and apparitions

atrophied **arteries** extending to the anterior brain

adrenaline **flooding** through fluid bodies

fight flight or **freeze** false

evidence **appears** real

Don' t **believe**

every thing

y o u

think

The Shame Game

Self   *All shook up*

       A shambles

            Complicated

               Confusing conundrum

Which way to go?

Can't remember
why you're spinning

Can't remember
anything

            Just whirling

            around

            and around

Glimpses of
sublime scenery
stroke the dewy casing of

         y o u r   e y e s

But sharp shards of
desert dirt

     b l u r your blue vision

Furiously scraping out sand
you hope to catch
a glimpse of truth

But you see only   backwards:
w a y before y e s t e r d a y
before you could
really r e m e m b e r

Over time you began
to s c h o o l yourself

in *separate-ness*

Believing you were wrong
utterly unworthy and unlovable

Sweet child   it is a lie
a fantasy   a fearful fairy-tale
Fodor
feeding false stories to
your sweet soft h e a r t

Wait until the spinning   stops
to wash away
this dusty delusion

Sit in sovereignty
and t o u c h your
sacred *serenity*

Sovereignty

Inside
a beacon
a sign
of self-sovereignty

Outside
restless rustlings of
foreign
wound-up words
make-believing wisdom

Lassoing
Limbs
Laughing

Desperate to destabilize
quiet surrender
to the heart

The heart

The place from which
to listen
and bathe one's self
in love

In love

Not
greedy grasping
for another

No
a visceral wisdom
a quiet voice

Porous People

Pulsing
         pulsing
porous   people

The ones who hold
their arms out
embrace our pain away

Porous   people

the ones
without waxy Teflon armour

No thermometer

No way to weigh
what *belongs*
to them
or to another

Mopping up moments
we so willingly
wash our hands of

They store them
in secret secure stashes
stockpiling
other people's stuff ...

Molecules of memories
a metaphoric bloating
merging our stories
with   their own

Powerless

That potent P word
sends sharp shivers
down the scaffolding
of the spine

When Pride pretends
it knows how to turn tides
talk others into Truths

Make molehills
into mountains

Why do we delude
ourselves into
dizziness?

Dancing circles around
the simple solution of surrender

What is so seductive
that nudges us
into nonsensical neurosis?

Beliefs that bully us
to believe we could somehow
orchestrate the outcome
of our life …

Under the Tree

Under
the tree
I see you
eyes open
an undeniable
mirror to
my secrets
the ones
I think
I have
but you
see them
I feel you
see them

You know
your seeing
takes them
places them
before me
an offering
of sorts

An un-
comfort-
table
unveiling
of my
humanity
exposed
alone
unable to
accept
my own
frailty

I frantically forage for twigs and sticks

Too blind to my own divinity

N o t
s e e i n g
I   r u n
t r i p p i n g
t u m b l i n g
t e r r i f i e d

Exhausted   I stop

pick the splinters
out of my eyes

M y   e y e s
o p e n
I   s e e   you
Y o u   a r e
n o t m e

The mystery of
my secrets
revealed through
healing eyes

My eyes

another's eyes
to see
my own

h u m a n i t y

Algorithms for Abundance

A plethora of
algorithms for
abundance

You'll find them
as your scroll your
never-ending newsfeed
furiously searching
for that one thing
to make it

alright   all right

Ten easy steps:

How to Live Your Life

Copious cups of crisp kale
squashed and squeezed
handfuls of dandelion leaves

How to Live Your Life

Walk – Run – Downward facing dog
burns through your mental fog

Next—

Meditate
to find
an ecstatic state

Simultaneously
socialize
theorize

Be still and …

Don't Stop

Behold the bounty
it beckons you
perched on a pot of gold
just at the edge

of a rainbow

Conspicuous Melancholy

It is always after
the very last dish is washed
and put away
when your teeth are brushed
and you've wiped away
the dirt of the day
when it's quiet
so very quiet

*

Faint echoes of today
bounce around
and yet your buoyancy
has gone

Bathed instead in
conspicuous melancholy
as night steps in

*

The death of the day
symbolic of
your aloneness

Startled
you look away
seeking something
to satisfy

to quench the thirsty quiet

*

A task
a telephone call
a new to-do-list
all temporary tranquilizers
until you listen

Listen
to the quiet
decide to nestle
into the comfort of
your own arms
the ones you were born with
the ones that have held another

They are strong
and forgiving

Trust them

The Silken Ground

On this day
you awoke again
marvelled in
your own divinity

Your gaze still
slightly clouded
with sleepiness

Yet you knew...

Somehow you knew
today was not like
yesterday

Today was a gift

Not the kind
to be furiously
unwrapped and
thrown away

No   today
as you sat up
in your sacred body
and your feet
met the silken ground

the lessons of
yesterday had
lingered just long enough
to transform
the trickery of
your mind

Your mind
your mischievous mind

You chuckled
knowing
tomorrow
was just another
sunset away

Like a Disco Ball

no rhyme   no reason   change of perception

reflections   of a disco ball   catching light spinning

so too   mixed moods   different views

seduction of   the mind   thinking   *this* is real

tomorrow   another chance   a new romance with a

different reality   spinning   so convincing until the

sun   comes up again   stillness   early light   a

moment of   a g l i m p s e   o f   n e u t r a l i t y

Puddles of Confusion

Perfect pictures
of your pristine life
instagrammable
inspirational

The Power of Positive Thinking

The answer to everything
perhaps yet don't delete
or undo   unmistakable
undeniable   but reliable
suffering a willingness
to sit in the mud
without your rubber boots

Naked feet
feeling frothy bubbles
umpteen puddles
of confusion wading your way
through your humanness
others' humanness

Hollow enough
to invite the earth in
through the soles of your feet

Let her wisdom
dwell in your cells
Listen to her
Listen to her

She knows your suffering
sees the other side
Trust her

Empty and Whole

Did someone ever tell you
it's silly to be sad
somehow sad is bad

Did you learn
to pull up your socks
pull yourself together

yank yourself
out of your sad slump
just stop being sad

What if
you soaked up
your sadness

sensed it
deep in your bones
let the molecules

in your marrow
make friends with
melancholy

What if
you listened to
music

so morose
it made you weep
your body heavy like a tree

thousands of tears
cascading down
down to its birthplace

The ground
your ground
the place that holds *you* up

Where you get to stand
after the storm
after the sadness

empty and whole

Tapestry

Strung together   the hours

silken threads   some soft to touch

yet sturdy enough   to withstand the strain

others   you   yourself roped together

tied in thick sailing knots   so secure

that untying them scalded you

made your hands bleed

Most moments   though

married by scraps and threads

you scavenged along the way

like surgically pieced-together

pipedreams and pauses

Your story flawlessly sews itself

into the tapestry of your life

Trust Your Gut

When you were little
someone cradled your skull
when flimsy words were not available
for all your wants and needs

You could not question
your thoughts and those of
your mother who just knew
when you were hungry
when you were lonely
when you were angry
when you were tired

Your birth had given you
the gift of knowing
a visceral thermometer
of basic needs and wants

When did you forget that?

When did you
            ignore
                    avoid
            circumvent
the gift of
        cellular knowledge
and replace it with
            a recklessness rebuff
                            of intuition?

How the Sun Strokes Your Skin

Quiet solitude

(an alternative to
noisy loneliness)

that tender
space of contented
aloneness where

I am

Is enough

S   m   i   l   e

Remember your small self
when you sat in
tall tall grass
warmed by the
sun stroking your skin

You watched
small creatures
go about their busy-ness
for hours on end

You   contented in your
quiet aloneness

Sometimes when we look so close
so close to finger out the fluff
from the centre of our navel
or when we stare so hard
to figure out how to walk
the wobbling Earth
what to think   how to say
where to stand   if it matters at all
The answers we seek
shapeshift into more
                    complex
            confused
conundrums
a veritable clusterfuck of questions

What to do   What to do

Turn to trusted travellers
the ones we walk with
the ones who see our suffering
and smile

Grateful for someone
to hold their hand
to interlock fingers with

Pull them away from the fluff
stuck deep inside their navel
the one they've been staring at

VII.
Expansions

Expand

What if it were possible to marry
all your senses   to breathe in
through the tips of your toes
hear echoes of sensation
on the surface of your skin
or through the sling of each eyeball?

What if only for a moment
you could touch the light inside of you
watch it expand and nudge you
into recognizing each moment—
so tenderly you could taste them
as your tongue settled in to kiss
the smoothness behind your teeth?

What if upon awakening
when your toes touch hard ground
tomorrow you invite breath in
straight through your toes?

Chose to Change Your Mind

When those pesky
little nit-picking
skin-crawling
serpents slither
their way into
your mental
machinery
as they hook
themselves around
copious crusty memories
feeding tangling trapping
ill-tempered habits to
make themselves
relevant *right now*

This time
change your mind
surrender the snakes
unshackle yourself
fix faulty wiring
find yourself free
from frivolous
fictitious
conviction

and sit
sit in the storm
sit like a mountain

in the menacing wind

The Choices We Make

In your reflection fiercely examine
the course of your life sketched
so skilfully across your face   forming
the structure of your aging scaffolding

lean in a little closer
softly stroke your fingers
along fine pathways
melting into each other

imprints of the life choices we make
painting passages   telling your treasured
tales to the world   some revealing
that not-so-secret-suffering
in the brushstrokes across your brow
others hug the dimples near your lips
long to lift up your rosy cheeks
and crease the corners of your eyes

A spectacular story!
Right here
in your reflection
the choices we make

It's That Time Again

After you've *finally* picked up
that damned key and jostled it
into its rightful hole (crossing
fingers that it won't fit) it fits

Some tender effort is required
to coax the key by dancing it
back and forth   not a click
more like a low thump

and the door floats open
effortlessly   offering you a vision
one you did not anticipate

There is no ground   There is no sky
There is nothing but vast open space
and a brightness that flimsy words
could not begin to describe

What will you do when you get there?

Will you find friends floating around
frolicking in the freedom of nothingness?

Will you be alone?

Will that matter?

Will there be a purpose
to this leg of the journey?

Will this place be
open and vacuous?

Or   if you peer ahead
can you see something?

Anything at all?

Does it matter?

Do you need the answer?

Can you be?—just be
in the bright powerful place
of nothing

trusting it is

e v e r y t h i n g

Habit

Our first encounter
you were the exhale
who caught my
never-ending inhale

You stroked my
heart and lungs
allowed them to heal

You were always with me
within arms' reach
to pacify my seductive
toxic thinking

Even stopped
tears from rolling
down my cheeks

Today I am stronger   *Thank you*

Today as I throw you into the light
a certain sadness washes over me

You were a good friend
but I must make the rest
of this journey without you

There are others with me
they will hold my hand
tightly sometimes—
but always with love

I am ready

Effervescent Anger

There are of course many ways
to meet the frothy monster

Some of us unwilling to look
into his bloodshot bulbous eyes
for fear of contagion

Others revel in his fiery fervour
nuzzle up against him
soak up and saturate ourselves
in his seething

Few of us feign indifference
to this furious fellow
sometimes held at bay
for years on end

The almost-forgotten and fiendish
finds a way to purge himself
and burst from our being
for no particular reason

B O O M

He's out! flailing around
like an untameable toddler's tantrum

Option 1

Quickly coax him back inside
smile furiously and hope no one was looking
Swallow him whole and bury him as he breathes

Option 2

Let him have at it
All of it
Everyone
Burn the house down

Option 3

See him
He is afraid
Just wants you to
hold his hand

hold his hand

hold his hand

Until the Crying Stops

Remember when you were little?—
when you fell down scraped your knees
on the gravel?—scuffed the heels
of your hands as you caught your fall?
Remember looking to your big person
wondering if it was okay to cry?—
wondering what would make you
a big person?—Remember how much work
it took to heave yourself away from the ground?
—as you realized "you're ok" and you brushed
yourself off pretending to believe it?
Remember the next time you fell
you were alone and there was no one to look to
and no one to tell you "you're ok"?
Remember how you took a deep deep
Breath "pulled yourself together"
and widened your eyes to stop the tears
streaming down your soft ruddy face?
Don't you wonder why you don't like to cry?
Why you cover your face to shield the glaring eyes of
other big people lest they know it hurts?
Don't you wonder why   when it's not ok
you tell the world it is?

Perhaps there are big people
willing to watch you cry
until the crying stops
because
it will

Just Another Day in Paradise

Last week
on that glorious sunny day
you had that moment

of remembering
your divinity—
felt the ground

support your steps
though   you were so light
you didn't need much help

You stood strong
breathed in the miracle
of your life

Spontaneous smiles
ricocheted and
reflected back to you

from perfect strangers
You stood
in your serenity

soaked up all that was
realizing everything
wanting nothing

Yesterday
on that glorious sunny day
you had that moment

of panic and paralysis
felt the weary weight
of your body

Each step
dragging your ball
and chain

you stood
in the heat of the day
laborious breaths

collapsing your lungs
into your heart
Passers-by

pitied you   judged you
your life
a confusing conundrum

Today
on this glorious sunny day
perhaps another miracle

a pondering
of life's purpose
Perhaps a day to pull

the covers over your head
or perhaps a day to
chortle at the painstaking

nit-picking
pontifications in your mind
perhaps *all* of this is

just another day
in paradise
Perfect!

It's Just Harder for You

As your mind begins
to investigate why
today has happened *again*

you realize
it's just harder for you
it's just not fair

Why is it that
life is so *difficult*
for you?

As you lie on your 300-
count sheets
your tummy full

and gurgling away
your take-out
teriyaki chicken don

you ponder
the lousy lot in your *life*
If they only knew

understood just
what you had been through
they'd shower you with

a t t e n t i o n
stroke your head
"There there …"

Then you'd feel better
You have pushed   prodded
and poked every pylon in your way

picked yourself up
Others' struggles pale in comparison
Poor you

It's just harder for you
Perhaps you haven't
told the right people

Perhaps you should
pick up the telephone
tell your tale to another

Pour your heart out
Point out where and how
It's just harder for you

Or perhaps you
could press your cheek
to your pillow

pray for another
peer into the darkness
until your eyes close

Your body
swaddled in sleepiness
the summary of today's

sorrows
slipping away into
slumber ....

Just Before the Solstice

On this dark dark day the heavens' offering
bathed us in beauty and when the sun briefly

stroked the ground it reflected the light
a foreshadowing of future days to come

Two more days two more days to embrace
the darkness   Consider caressing it

be courageous enough to wait
for the light to weave its way back in

Watch though as you want it to hurtle itself
at you   as you want it to storm your life

to shine so brightly as if to burn away
the beauty of the darkness

Gather all your grace and surrender
surrender to the winter of your life

It may be your truest teacher

Listen

Another Revolution

Spinning around
and around

            you find yourself
            here again

inching closer to
another

            spin
            sequence

Your beating heart
nestled neatly

            in the cocoon of
            your breathing body

standing firmly
on the ground

            The ground
            layer-

caked around
this sphere

            you stand on
            spinning

around and around
you sometimes unsure

if your *own* spinning
is the catalyst for

        global gyrations
        you chuckle

at your mind's
capacity for chicanery

        You prepare yourself
        to spin again

Around
and around

        decide to delight
        in the spinning

watch the whirling
disco ball of days

        as they are delivered
        one by one

Morning Glory

Look out your window
as liquid gold
drapes itself across
the horizon and
folds over the
edges of the world

Watch the orchestra
of winged creatures
as they crescendo
soaring higher
and higher
stealing tiny
drops of ore
to feed their
hungry offspring

Listen
listen to their
morning lullaby
as it lures you
out of your slumber
and reminds you to
wake up
and drink up
the nectar of
this morning glory

Picking Through the Rubble

Stepping
over the threshold

a compulsion came
over you

a compulsion
to stare

behind
yourself

You became
your very own

private investigator
leafing through

the stories of
your life

picking through
crumpled

crusty pieces
to toss them

over your shoulder
finding

evidence
clues of tangible memories

a collage
of misdemeanours

making up a manual of
what not to do

an old man
with a cigarette

in his mouth mumbled
Look   but don't stare

You wondered
whether he spoke

from experience
whether the nicotine

dripping from his lips
was his death-wish

whether he had
stared for too long

You weren't willing
to chance it

taking one last
furtive glance

behind yourself
You shivered

shook free
the shackles

and stood in today's
promise for tomorrows

and waited

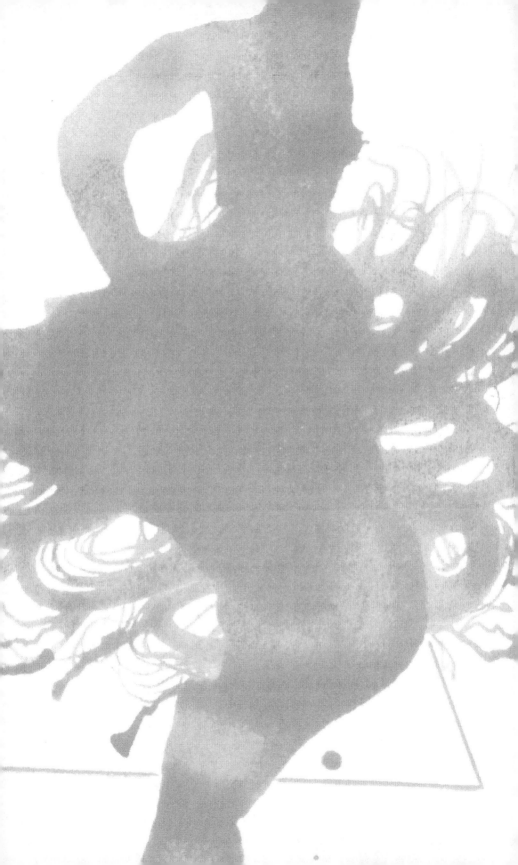

About the Author

Born to Swiss and British parents in Hong Kong where she spent her early childhood years, Dominique's thirst and talent for artistic expression brought her to the Elmhurst School for classical ballet in England. While on the surface a privileged and prestigious opportunity open to only a select few, being sent a half a world away was a life of rigid structure, unceasing criticism, and unbridled and ruthless competition for perfection. This was one of many traumatic turning points in young Dominique's experience, revealing an intrinsic fear of imperfection and abandonment that had remained a constant through adolescence and well into adulthood. The family moved to affluent Greenwich, Connecticut, where Dominique found an abundance of easily available ways to drown her insecurities and fit in. She graduated from high school to pursue a bachelor's degree at Boston University, but left early to work in the family trading business in Switzerland. In her late twenties, Dominique moved to Montreal, Canada, where she married and had two children.

Dominique lives in Vancouver, British Columbia. She is a devoted student and yoga teacher. Her own healing journey through yoga, ignited her passion to bring that possibility to others. Her work has led her to teach in addiction centres and hospitals, offering yoga as part of an holistic treatment for trauma and addiction.

Formed by her punishing and instructed personal journey to tame her own demons, Dominique Vincenz's poetry is a raw and sometimes wrenching mirror on her lifelong pursuit for understanding and healing.

This is the first time her immensely private works have been published. They are at times wrenching, sobering, funny, and always compelling. Among other themes, Dominique's poetry is a full frontal attack on the notion that physical beauty and technical mastery in any endeavour is the ticket to acceptance and love. Her search for truth, meaning and authenticity is the thematic anchor for her poetry and how she is commited to live her life.

www.dominiquevincenz.com

About the Cover Artist

Shirley Wiebes' diverse practice encompasses drawing, photography, sculpture and song writing. A self-taught artist, she shifts fluidly between materials and media, continually bringing an innovative approach to both subject and matter.

Her early work focused on small clay based human forms that exuded vitality and empowerment. Assemblage and site-specific installation utilizing found objects and commonplace materials followed. Drawing and song writing are ongoing immediate vehicles for developing and expressing narrative. Human geography and the connection between people and place form a continuous thread in all these explorations.

Wiebes' recent work considers transformation in both the natural and built environment with series such as *FLATLANDS*, 2015 examining the Canadian prairies and *TRACES DIARY*, 2017 documenting Vancouver's rapid development. Here she merges photographic image with mixed media, blurring the boundary between picture and drawing, real and imagined space. Her work suggests there is mystery in the ordinary and the viewer is left to redefine what seems familiar.

www.shirleywiebe.com